HAPPY TIME

(On S'Amuse Au Piano)

by ALEXANDRE TANSMAN

Contents

ISBN: 978-1-4234-1530-5

HAL•LEONARD®
CORPORATION
7777 W. BLUEMOUND RD. P.O. BOX 13819 MILWAUKEE, WI 53213

Visit Hal Leonard Online at
www.halleonard.com

A la Schumann
A la Schumann

Alexandre Tansman

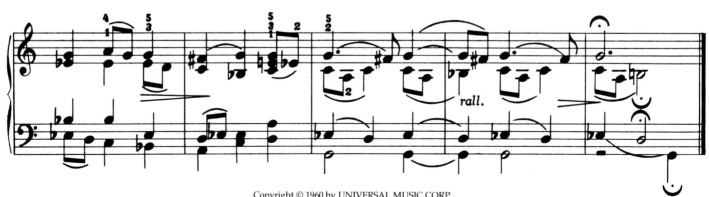

Organ
Orgues

Alexandre Tansman

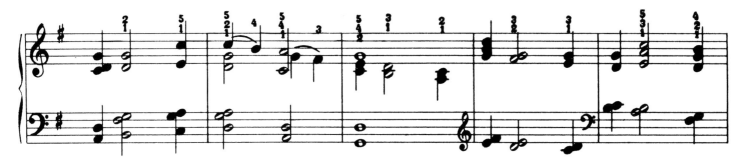

Little Game
Petit Jeu

Alexandre Tansman

Light Waltz
Valse Légère

Alexandre Tansman

Night Mood
Nocturne

Alexandre Tansman

Moderato

pp sempre, dolce

lontano

rall. - - - - - - - -

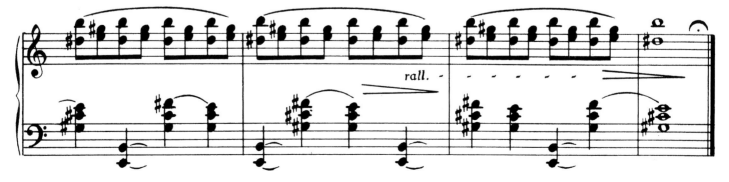

Arioso, alla J.S. Bach

Alexandre Tansman

Oriental Dance
Danse d'Orient

Alexandre Tansman

Iberian Mood
Echo Ibérique

Alexandre Tansman

In Memory of George Gershwin "1925"

Alexandre Tansman

* On repeat go to the last measure.

Finale, Solo-Piece
Pièce Finale

Alexandre Tansman

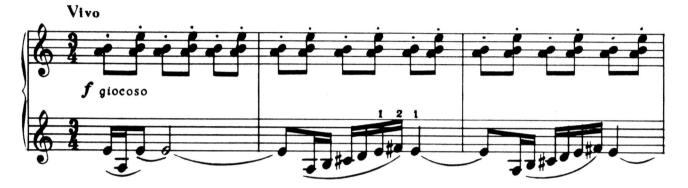